How to make and fly
Paper planes

How to make and fly
Paper planes

Nick Robinson

p

This is a Parragon Publishing Book
This edition published in 2003

Parragon Publishing
Queen Street House
4 Queen Street
Bath BA1 1HE, UK

ISBN 1-40542-003-0

Cover design by Red Central

Printed in China

Contents

An Introduction to Paper Planes   **6**
A Brief History of Flight   8
How and Why Planes Fly   12
Making Your Own Planes   15
Flying Competitively   19

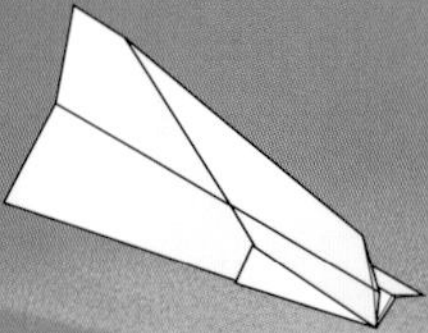

Classic Designs   **23**
Classic Dart   24
Hawk Dart   26
Classic Glider   30
Keel Plane   32

Modern Designs   **37**
Barnstormer   38
Triplane   42
Norton Flyer   46
Renishaw   48

Space Age Designs   **53**
Seed Floater   54
Space Fighter   56
Roller Blade   58
Whizzer   60

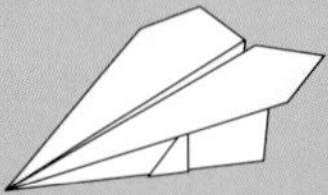

Glossary of Aviation Terms   62

Index   63

Acknowledgements   64

Introduction

An Introduction to Paper Planes

Paper planes are fun to make, and making them is not only an exciting hobby but it is also one that could lead to greater things. In this introduction, Chris Edge, who holds the current world record for the longest flight of a paper plane, explains what you do once you have perfected the designs in this book.

The first step would be to get together with some friends and to see who has managed to make the best design.

When it comes to a flying competition, there are really only two choices available to you: to see whose plane flies the furthest (known as a distance competition) or to see whose plane flies for the longest time (known as a duration competition).

Distance competitions are comparatively easy to arrange. All you need is the use of a long room, such as a school hall. Agree on the number of flights each of you will make, mark a line on the floor and take turns to launch your planes from behind that line. As each plane lands, mark its position on the floor.

Duration contests are a little more difficult to organize because you need a high-ceilinged room, such as a sports hall. Again, agree on the number of flights each of you will make and use a stopwatch to time the plane from the moment it is thrown until the moment it lands. The plane that is in the air the longest time is the winner.

I have been mainly involved in duration competitions, and I am currently joint world record holder for the longest indoor flight with a paper plane. The record time – 20.9 seconds – was set in July 1996 in an aircraft hangar at Cardington, Bedfordshire, and it beat the previous record, which had been held for many years by American Ken Blackburn. The plane I used was a simple design, similar to many of those in the book, but I have perfected it through trial and error and some science for more than two years.

Both distance and duration contests enable you to experiment with different designs. One of the most appealing aspects of making paper planes is that you can work quickly, and if they don't work, you can just throw the paper into the recycling bin and

start again. In just a few minutes you could find that you have a world-beating design.

When you are beginning to make paper planes for a competition, bear the following points in mind. First, start with a proven design – many of the planes shown in this book are ideal. Make your planes carefully, taking trouble to fold the paper exactly as shown and starting again with fresh paper if you make a mistake. When you are making the folds, make sure they are crisp by running your fingernail along them. Sharp, neat folds will help the plane to fly. When you have finished making the plane, do a few gentle test throws and adjust the wings to see if you can improve the flight pattern. Then try some harder throws, but continue to make small adjustments to the design.

I always look forward to duration contests. I never know if the planes I will be making are going to be world beaters, but it's great fun trying. Who knows? You may find yourself folding a record-beating plane and, like me, you may end up on television.

Good luck and good throwing.

Chris Edge, London

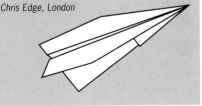

A Brief History of Flight

Although the history of manned flight is well known, no one knows for certain where or when the first paper airplanes were flown. They may well have been discovered in Ancient Egypt when papyrus was first discovered.

Paper kites are known to have been made in China over 2000 years ago, but the Greek philosopher Aristotle (384–322 BC) was the first to write down his theories of how and why things flew, although he got several things wrong.

The Italian polymath Leonardo da Vinci (1452–1519) thought that the up-and-down movement of a bird's wings was the key to flying, and he developed plans for what is known as an 'ornithopter'. We now know that this type of aircraft is not practicable, although working toys are possible. He also drew diagrams of what must have been a type of helicopter many hundreds of years before the real thing took to the air. He is thought to have experimented with parchment planes to help work out the principles of flight.

Another three hundred years passed before the English scientist Sir George Cayley (1773–1857) developed what were to become the basic principles of flight as we know them. He experimented with a number of gliders and helicopters and realized the importance of tilting the wings slightly upwards to make a plane more stable by creating a dihedral angle (see page 18). His work on

A Malayasian kite and its maker.

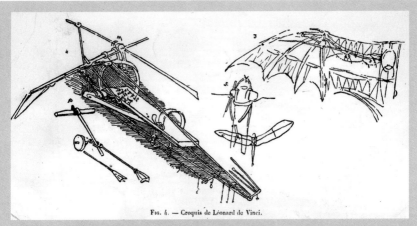

FIG. 4. — Croquis de Léonard de Vinci.

Drawings from the sketchbook of Leonardo da Vinci, 1508

making something that was heavier than air fly might well have been ignored by a sceptical public but for the invention of the manned balloon by people such as the French Montgolfier brothers. They used paper to make hot air balloons, and their first manned balloons, which flew in 1783 were made from cloth lined with paper.

The Aeronautical Society of Great Britain was formed in 1866, and at about the same time the German Otto Lilienthal (1848–96) and his brother were developing gliders capable of carrying a man. They discovered that wings with a curved surface had much more lift than those with flat surfaces. Lilienthal also made the first rudimentary rudder, but he was killed in 1896 during a test flight. An Englishman, Percy Pilcher had

flown in a Lilienthal glider, and he extended his work to include a wheeled undercarriage. He was in the process of designing an aero-engine when a tail failed, causing his death.

The first 'proper' flight of a real airplane was made in America by the Wright brothers on 17th December 1903 at Kitty Hawk, North Carolina, and it is possible that they may have seen and used paper airplanes. To this day, the best way of learning about the basic principles of flight is to experiment with sheets of paper.

The primitive biplanes gave way to high powered monoplanes in the late 1930s. During this exciting period the American John Northrop (1895–1981) used paper

9

The Wright brothers attempting a precarious landing

airplanes to test his ideas for flying winged aircraft. Those humble paper airplanes may well have played a small part in the eventual development of the Stealth bomber!

The Second World War led to a massive surge in the development of flight technology. From 1939, when biplanes were still in common use, aircraft developed into rocket- and jet-powered designs, capable of near supersonic flight. German scientists in particular explored many strange and advanced designs, including delta wings and asymmetrical designs. After the war the Americans developed many of their ideas, leading to the first supersonic flight by Charles 'Chuck' Yeager (b. 1923) in 1947 flying a Bell X-1 The speed of sound is 331m (1087ft) per second at sea level. This speed is known as Mach 1. Twice the speed of sound is Mach 2 and so on.

Since 1947, airplanes have become faster and flown higher. The first practical VTOL (vertical take-off and landing) airplane was developed in England during the 1950s and is still in use today in the form of the Harrier jump jet. As the race for space began, planes flew to the outer edges of our atmosphere to learn how a design might work in space as well as in our own atmosphere. The NASA space shuttle is the end result of these early experiments and is a perfect combination of airplane and space craft. Designs are currently being created for larger space-going aircraft that may one day take people to distant planets.

NASA space shuttle 'Discovery' lifts off

How and Why Planes Fly

When we talk about something flying, we mean that it stays in the air for a reasonable time and behaves in a predictable way. There are two types of flight: powered (with an engine of some kind) and gliding. Paper planes fall into the second category! Luckily for us, the same principles that allow a powered airplane to fly also apply to paper airplanes. We can also use paper to explain these principles.

If you drop a sheet of paper to the floor, it twists and turns in a random way. Technically, this type of flight is called unstable. If we form the paper into the shape of a cone using sticky tape or a staple, the flight pattern changes dramatically. It now falls smoothly to the floor and will always fall in the same direction. The flight is more stable and predictable. The more tightly you roll the cone, the faster it will fall because it can slip through the air more easily.

If you drop the cone and a sheet of paper at the same time, the cone will land first, because it meets less air resistance. The main factor that creates resistance is having a bulky shape, although the density of the object (how solid it is) has an effect as well. A streamlined shape will create less resistance and so fly more smoothly. This is why fast cars and airplanes have smooth profiles: they can slice through the air more

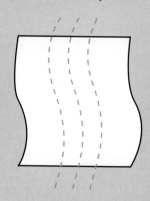

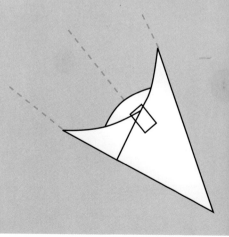

easily and meet less resistance. We can easily design our planes so that they are streamlined, but they also need to stay in the air longer than the cone does. To do this, we must create lift.

Experiments by the early pioneers showed that we can provide lift by putting a slight curve in a wing. This is explained by Bernoulli's Principle, which says that air pressure around a surface decreases as the speed of the air increases.

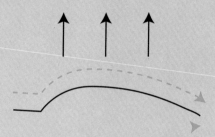

If we make a curve in the paper, air flowing over it will have to move faster over the top of a curved wing, because it has further to travel. This will create a lower air pressure on the upper surface and the wing will tend to rise. This is how we create lift. You can test this principle by holding a strip of paper with the short end near your mouth. If you blow over the top of the paper, it rises. This is because the increase in speed lowers the air pressure, creating lift.

A powered airplane will use an engine to reach speeds that give it enough lift to stay in the air. Because a paper plane is quite slow, (and we can't easily add a curve to the wing), it cannot stay in the air for much longer than 20 seconds in the best of conditions. We must make the best use of this time.

The amount of lift is also affected by the dihedral or the angle at which the wing meets the air. This is known as the angle of attack. A shallow angle provides the most lift, which is why airplanes take off and land at a gentle angle. If a wing meets the air at a steep angle, the lift will reduce until it is less than the force of gravity trying to pull it down again. When this happens we say the airplane is stalling. We want our plane to meet the air at the correct angle. This will be different for each design.

Stability in flight

For distance flights, we want our plane to fly in a fixed direction, whereas for the maximum time in the air, a gentle curve is better. In order to achieve either of these targets, the plane must not change the way in which it flies – it must be stable. In a real aircraft the pilot uses control surfaces, such as the rudder and aileron, to control the plane's stability. There are three possible ways in which a plane can turn.

Roll

If one wing goes down as the other goes up, the plane will roll. The pilot uses the aileron (see Glossary) to prevent rolling. On a paper plane, we adjust the angle of the wings.

Pitch

If the back of the plane falls as the nose rises (or vice versa) the plane will pitch. The pilot uses the elevators (see Glossary) to prevent pitching. On a paper plane, we adjust the paper at the back of the wings.

Yaw

If one wing moves further forward as the other moves backwards, the plane will yaw. The pilot uses the rudder to prevent yawing.

On a paper plane, we adjust the paper at the back of the body or the fuselage.

Although we can make some adjustments, the basic flight pattern is determined by the point around which the plane balances, which is known as the centre of gravity. If we suspended a plane by a single thread, it would balance, but only if the thread were attached at the centre of gravity. This point is determined by the final arrangement of the layers of paper. If the centre of gravity is correct, the plane will make a successful flight more often than not. Tests have shown that the ideal centre of gravity is towards the front of the plane. Most paper planes therefore have more paper at the front to make this the heavier end.

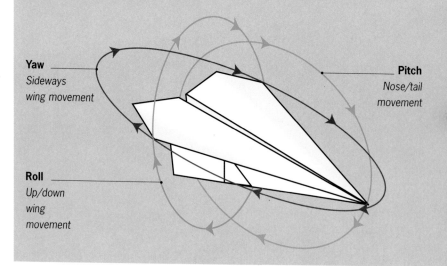

Yaw
Sideways wing movement

Pitch
Nose/tail movement

Roll
Up/down wing movement

Making Your Own Planes

**Paper is one of the simplest materials to work with.
It is cheap and widely available, and you can choose from a huge range
of colours and patterns. Most paper planes are made from rectangles
(although some use a square), and we can find suitable paper almost
everywhere we look. Photocopy paper is ideal, and you can buy packets
of it very cheaply. Most paper-folders are always on the look-out
for free samples and make good use of leaflets that may be
pushed through their letterboxes.**

When we make paper planes, we should use fresh paper of medium weight. Thicker paper works nearly as well, but might not fly very well if the model is too heavy. Thin paper can lose its shape when you launch it. Paper that has been left in the open for a long time can absorb moisture from the air and becomes 'floppy', and this prevents it from flying very well. Cheaper types of paper, such as 'rice' or 'sugar' paper are suitable for trial runs, but not for the real thing. Once you have mastered the folding method, you might want to look for some brightly patterned paper for a really special plane. You can always decorate it yourself with pencils and crayons.

If a design starts with a square, you can either use origami paper or cut your own. Specialist paper comes in a variety of exciting finishes and can give your plane a very professional look, but it can be expensive. Making squares from rectangles is very easy and you can then use the same type of paper for all your designs.

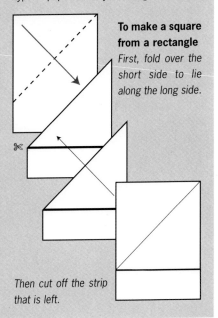

To make a square from a rectangle
First, fold over the short side to lie along the long side.

Then cut off the strip that is left.

The section of paper left over is almost the same shape as an American dollar bill. Paper plane experts like Stephen Weiss have invented a number of paper planes designed to use this shape. Why not see if you can invent one of your own?

Folding technique

When you start folding it's a good idea to use a table or other flat surface to fold on. If you are new to paper-folding, you should also stop between folds and look at the next diagram. Before creasing, check the paper is lined up exactly. If you get it wrong you can refold it, but the old creases may make life harder and the plane fly worse.

If a fold is easier made by turning the paper around or (with mountain folds) upside down, feel free to move it to the best position, but don't forget to return it afterwards so that it corresponds to the next diagram. Accurate folding also needs a neat rectangle (or square) to start with.

Using the instructions

The planes in this book are arranged with the easiest first, so you are recommended to fold through them in order. The diagrams show you a series of steps that end up with the finished plane. You must follow these steps in the order shown! It's also useful to look ahead to the next step each time, so you know what you are aiming for.

The first diagram will show creases already on the paper. These are always 'half-way' creases, made by folding the paper in half.

Symbols

Paper-folding diagrams use a series of standard origami symbols so that they can be read by anyone, regardless of language. The two basic creases are a valley fold, indicated by a dotted line, and a mountain fold (sometimes called a 'peak' fold), indicated by alternating dots and dashes.

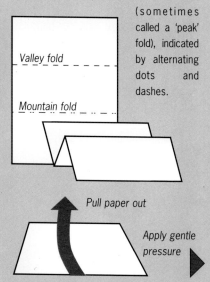

Valley fold

Mountain fold

Pull paper out

Apply gentle pressure

Other common symbols include 'pull the paper out', 'turn over the paper' and 'apply gentle pressure'.

Once you become familiar with the symbols, you will be able to make origami designs from anywhere in the world. If you invent your own plane, use the same symbols to make some instructions and send it to the British Origami Society whose address is at the end of this book.

Creating your own designs

The best way to create is to experiment with basic designs. Change the position of a crease and see how it affects the finished plane. Add extra folds, miss out folds – you don't have to follow the diagrams! Keep an open mind – some quite unlikely looking designs fly very well. Your plane doesn't have to be a typical glider, it might be a UFO or a Stealth bomber. Try to be different: you might want to make something that spins like a frisbee or a helicopter – the sky's the limit!

Flight adjustments

There are three major factors that affect the flight of a paper airplanes: the angle of launch, the speed of launch and the dihedral.

Angle of launch

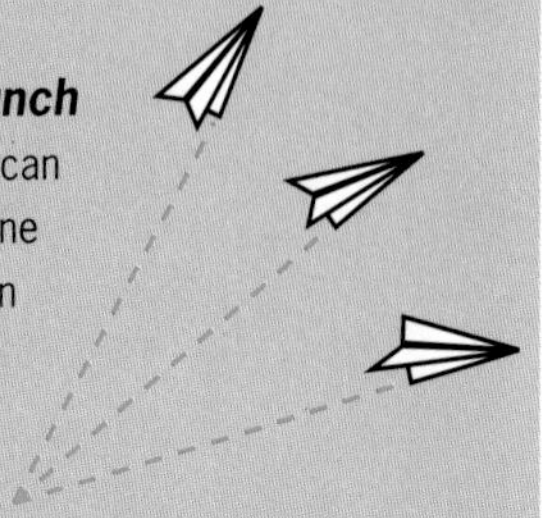

In theory you can launch the plane in any direction from down at the floor to straight up in the air.

In practice, however, each plane will have quite a limited range of angles if you want the best flight. Start by launching it forwards and slightly down, then note the flight pattern and try again with a slightly different angle. Try a wide range of angles to see which is best for your plane.

Speed of launch

Some planes fly best when launched slowly, others need a faster launch. Experiment to find the best.

Top ten tips for folding paper planes.

1. Try to find somewhere quiet so you can concentrate.
2. Set aside 'folding time' so you won't feel rushed.
3. Use a table or flat surface to fold on.
4. Make sure your hands are clean.
5. Fold slowly and carefully, making sharp and accurate creases.
6. Look ahead to the next diagram to see what you're aiming for.
7. Try not to put in 'extra' creases – they will affect the flight.
8. Never launch your plane towards anybody.
9. Don't give up if it doesn't fly properly.
10. Be prepared to experiment.

Dihedral

A paper plane is likely to roll, pitch or yaw or any combination of the three, but the biggest problem is often the pitch. We can control this by adjusting the dihedral or angle of the wings relative to the horizontal.

To give our planes dihedral, we fold the wings so that they both point upwards slightly. As one wing is lowered, the lift on the other wing is reduced, causing the plane

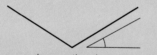

Always make sure the wings are at the same angle

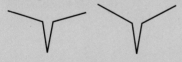

Try different dihedrals for each design

to move back to a more stable position. The angle of the wings will vary for each design When altering the dihedral, always try to make sure both wings have the same angle, or the plane will tend to roll.

As you might expect, these three factors affect each other. For instance, increasing the dihedral may mean you have to launch more slowly. After a while, you will learn to predict how this happens and adjust accordingly. Be patient and try to work out what is happening during the flight.

Fine tuning

Small changes to the trailing edge of the wings can have a large effect on the flight. Try to curl the paper very gently each time, in case it makes things worse! By deliberately making large curls, you can turn the plane into a barnstorming model, which performs spectacular aerobatics.

Weight

Some planes will work better if they are made from large sheets of paper, others are better made from small sheets. If the paper is too light, it will be blown by the wind too easily. If it is too heavy, it may not fly at all. The only way to find out is to experiment.

Height

If your plane is a glider rather than an acrobatic barnstormer, it will work better if you launch it from high up, such as from a bedroom window. Make sure you don't attempt to launch yourself!

Flying Competitively

Two main categories are recognized internationally: time aloft and distance. Many competitions extend this list to include a category for acrobatics and design, but the event centres around the 'big two'. Since the early days of competition both time and distance have steadily been improved upon, and they currently stand at 20.9 seconds in the air and 58.8m (193ft) distance.

The fragile nature of paper flight means that competitions must be held indoors where there are few air currents. Launches made outdoors might produce artificially good or poor results depending on how much wind was blowing that day and in what direction!

Various techniques and theories have been developed for each category.

Time aloft

The basic principle is to throw/launch the plane straight upwards as high as you can. It will then – ideally – begin a slow, circling descent. You will be limited by the height of the ceiling and the width of the area, so it's unlikely you will break any records unless you are in a large indoor stadium of some kind. You also have to be quite flexible to throw straight upwards – try it!

Your design should be adjusted so that as soon as the plane reaches its highest point, it immediately levels out. Any height lost will mean a shorter time in the air. Once it has levelled out, your plane should have a slight imbalance so that it starts to turn in a wide circle. Ideally, this circle will be a few feet smaller than the width of the arena.

Professional paper plane makers will make minute adjustments to their basic design to try to get the widest possible turning circle. The end result will need a slice of luck, since the paper will never behave the same way twice.

Distance

The distance in question is measured from the place where you launch the plane to the point where it first touches the ground. You will only get good results if your plane is trimmed to fly in a straight line. If it flies in a circle it may well travel a long way, but may not land very far away (as the crow flies). There are two ways to achieving long distance – the missile approach and the gliding approach.

The missile approach

This is quite a crude method, involving mostly brute force. You choose a streamlined design, then hurl it as fast as possible. Since you could do the same with a screwed-up ball of paper, many contests don't allow anything that looks too much like a missile.

The gliding approach

This is where you use the plane's natural flight characteristics to achieve distance. Some competitions have a category in which you release the plane from a fixed height – in other words, you don't give it any forward thrust. This allows children to compete on the same basis as adults, because physical strength isn't an issue.

The mixed approach

In practice, the most successful contestants will use strength to get the plane started, then allow it to glide for the remainder of the distance. If you launch a plane too quickly, the wings may buckle and reduce both stability and lift. Remember, speed and angle of launch affect each other.

Preparation is the key

If you want to enter a contest, you must put in plenty of practise! You need to be reasonably fit to compete with the best and practise will build up your muscles; you'd be surprised how much your arms can ache after a few hours enthusiastic launching! As well as being fit, you must know how to adjust your design for the best result. You will only have a few attempts in a contest, so it's vital you can watch your first flight, work out what needs changing and then make those changes.

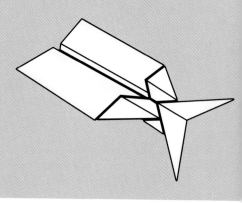

Current record holders are (at the time of writing)
Time aloft

Guinness World Record	20.9 seconds set by Chris Edge & Andy Currey 28 July 1996
Guinness British Record	20.9 seconds set by Chris Edge & Andy Currey 28 July 1996
Origami Record	20.9 seconds set by Andy Currey 28 July 1996

Distance

Guinness World Record	58.8m (193ft) set by Tony Fletch 21 May 1985
Guinness British Record	31.7m (104ft) set by Andy Currey 19 September 1997
Origami Record	28.7m (94ft) set by Robin Glynne 19 September 1997

If you decide to have a go at the record, you must have a clear video of your efforts; it isn't enough to have somebody as a witness – unless they are from the *Guinness Book of Records*! You will also need a room over 61m (200ft) long.

RULES

As you can imagine, there are lots of rules to abide by. Although you are allowed to used a small piece of sticky tape to hold your design together, many people try to use 'pure' origami methods. Here are the key rules from the **Guinness Book of Records.**

- *The record is for the duration or distance of an indoor paper airplane flight*

- *If your plane touches anything when in flight (including people, wall and roofing) that is then end of that flight*

- *The airplane must be made from one sheet of paper, using A4 or USA letter size paper*

- *The weight of the paper must be no more than 100 gsm (grams per square metre)*

- *The paper can be cut but any piece of paper cut off can't be joined back on again*

- *Standard clear sticky tape is allowed, but no longer than 3cm (1¹/₈in) on any one airplane*

- *The tape can be cut into smaller pieces but used only to hold down folds, not as a weight or to control the flight*

- *Glue is not allowed*

- *Ten attempts at the record are allowed*

- *The airplane should be flown by one person, from a reasonably fixed position. This means a long run up as part of the launch is not allowed*

- *When launching, your feet should not intentionally lift off the ground. The launch height is the height of the thrower, wearing normal footwear. No stilts!*

- *Distance throwers should not touch or cross over the launching line*

Classic Designs

To become a 'classic', like the Spitfire, a paper airplane must have stood the test of time. These designs have done just that and have been enjoyed by many thousands of people. These are simple yet elegant paper planes and you will be able to teach them to your friends.

Classic Dart

This tried-and-tested design is one of the simplest to make, but also one of the best! Nobody knows how old it is, but people all over the world have made it and enjoyed flying it.

1 Start with a sheet of A4, creased in half lengthways. Fold in two corners to lie along the centre crease.

2 Take the folded edges in to the centre as well.

3 Fold the paper plane in half.

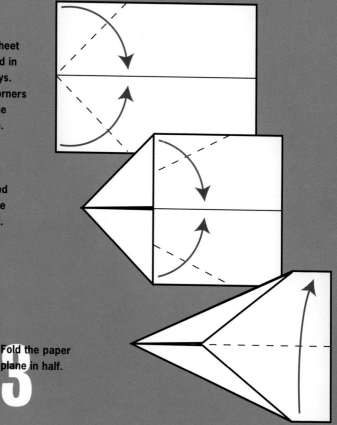

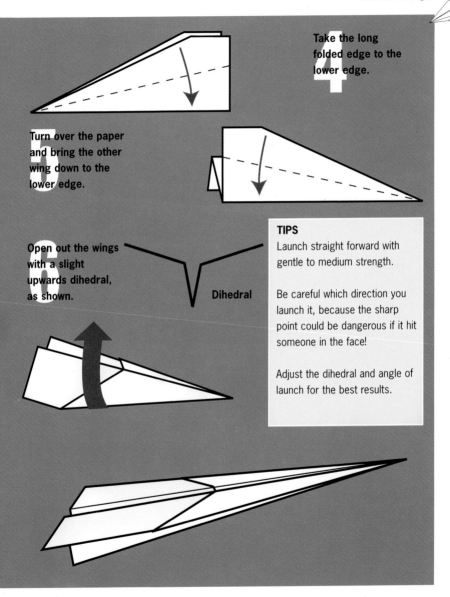

Take the long
folded edge to the
lower edge.

4

Turn over the paper
and bring the other
wing down to the
lower edge.

5

Open out the wings
with a slight
upwards dihedral,
as shown.

6

Dihedral

TIPS

Launch straight forward with
gentle to medium strength.

Be careful which direction you
launch it, because the sharp
point could be dangerous if it hit
someone in the face!

Adjust the dihedral and angle of
launch for the best results.

Hawk Dart

This traditional model is a superb glider, and although it looks very complex it isn't. It will also fly without the pleats. Some folders cut off the rear of the plane and make it into a narrow tailplane. It looks good, but will not fly as well.

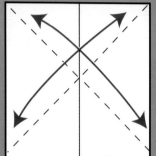

1 Start with a rectangle, creased in half lengthways. Fold a short edge over to the adjoining long edge. Crease firmly and unfold. Do the same with the other corner of the short edge.

2 Turn over the paper, then fold the shorter edge to meet the lower ends of the diagonals you have just made. Crease firmly and unfold.

3 Turn over again. Using the creases you have made, carefully collapse the paper towards you. The horizontal crease 'breaks' in the centre.

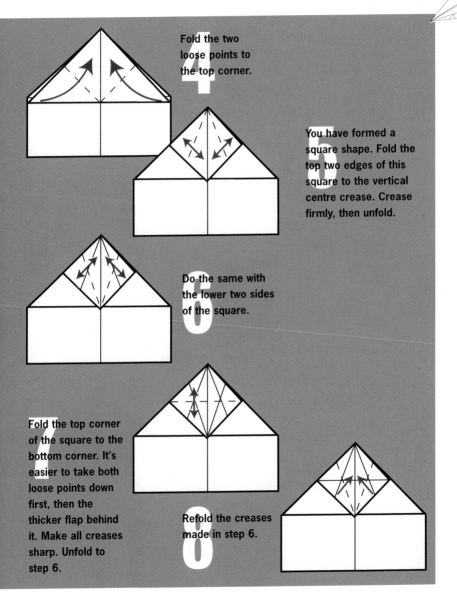

Fold the two
loose points to
the top corner.

You have formed a
square shape. Fold the
top two edges of this
square to the vertical
centre crease. Crease
firmly, then unfold.

Do the same with
the lower two sides
of the square.

Fold the top corner
of the square to the
bottom corner. It's
easier to take both
loose points down
first, then the
thicker flap behind
it. Make all creases
sharp. Unfold to
step 6.

Refold the creases
made in step 6.

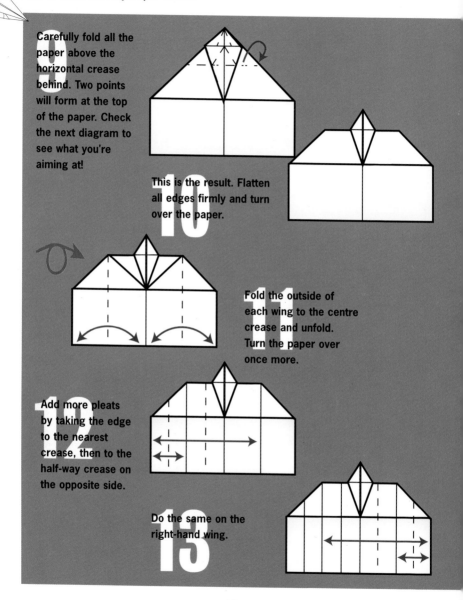

9 Carefully fold all the paper above the horizontal crease behind. Two points will form at the top of the paper. Check the next diagram to see what you're aiming at!

10 This is the result. Flatten all edges firmly and turn over the paper.

11 Fold the outside of each wing to the centre crease and unfold. Turn the paper over once more.

12 Add more pleats by taking the edge to the nearest crease, then to the half-way crease on the opposite side.

13 Do the same on the right-hand wing.

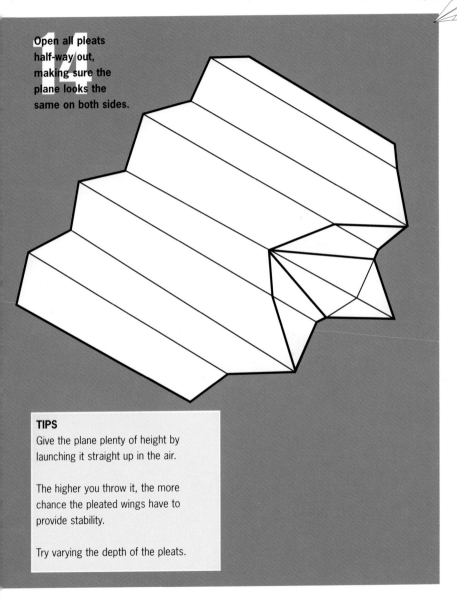

14 Open all pleats half-way out, making sure the plane looks the same on both sides.

TIPS

Give the plane plenty of height by launching it straight up in the air.

The higher you throw it, the more chance the pleated wings have to provide stability.

Try varying the depth of the pleats.

Classic Glider

This is a well-known design, which represents a step forward from the classic dart. It uses a technique developed by the paper plane expert Eiji Nakamura to hold the loose fuselage flaps firmly in place. This move takes place in step 5. This is one of the designs for which there is a template supplied. Use the template as a guide to making this plane.

1 Start with a sheet of A4, creased in half lengthways. Fold in two corners to lie along the centre crease.

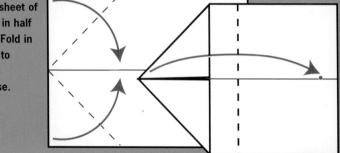

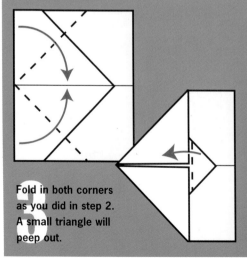

2 Fold the left-hand corner across to just short of the right hand edge. Make sure that the point lies on the centre crease. Check the next diagram to see what you're aiming at.

3 Fold in both corners as you did in step 2. A small triangle will peep out.

4 Fold back the triangle across the two corners. This holds the loose flaps in place when the plane is in flight.

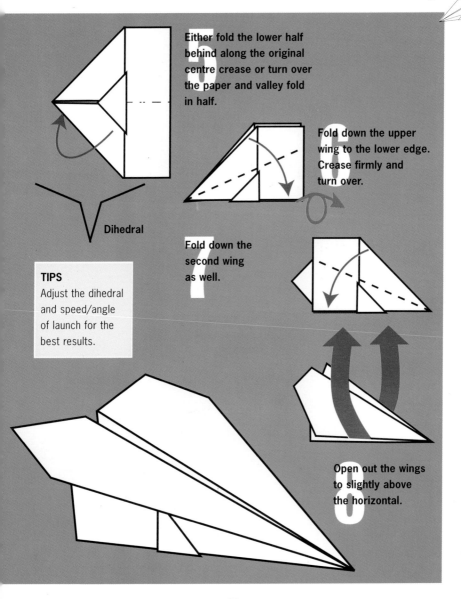

5 Either fold the lower half behind along the original centre crease or turn over the paper and valley fold in half.

Dihedral

6 Fold down the upper wing to the lower edge. Crease firmly and turn over.

7 Fold down the second wing as well.

TIPS
Adjust the dihedral and speed/angle of launch for the best results.

8 Open out the wings to slightly above the horizontal.

31

Keel Plane

This design is a variation on a traditional design and although it is very simple, it flies well. If you can fold the plane without problems, you might like to try the small variation that holds the fuselage together. This is an example of how a little thought and a few experiments can improve a basic design. Look at the other planes in this book and see if you can improve them!

1 Start with a rectangle, creased in half lengthways. Fold a short edge over to the adjoining long edge. Crease firmly and unfold. Do the same with the other corner of the short edge.

2 Turn over the paper, then fold the shorter edge to meet the lower ends of the diagonals you have just made. Crease firmly and unfold.

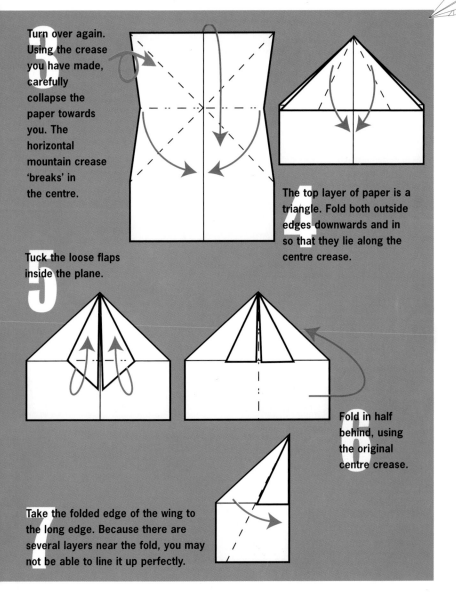

3 Turn over again. Using the crease you have made, carefully collapse the paper towards you. The horizontal mountain crease 'breaks' in the centre.

4 The top layer of paper is a triangle. Fold both outside edges downwards and in so that they lie along the centre crease.

5 Tuck the loose flaps inside the plane.

6 Fold in half behind, using the original centre crease.

7 Take the folded edge of the wing to the long edge. Because there are several layers near the fold, you may not be able to line it up perfectly.

33

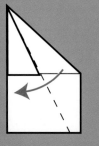

Turn over and fold the other wing in the same way.

Open out both wings to just above the horizontal.

TIPS
Launch straight forwards, firmly, from a point just in front of your head.

Try launching slightly faster or slower and see how this affects the flight path.

Variation

10 Unfold the design back to step 5 and fold the right hand flap inside as before. Pull out the hidden paper on the left hand side. Check the next diagram to see what you're aiming at.

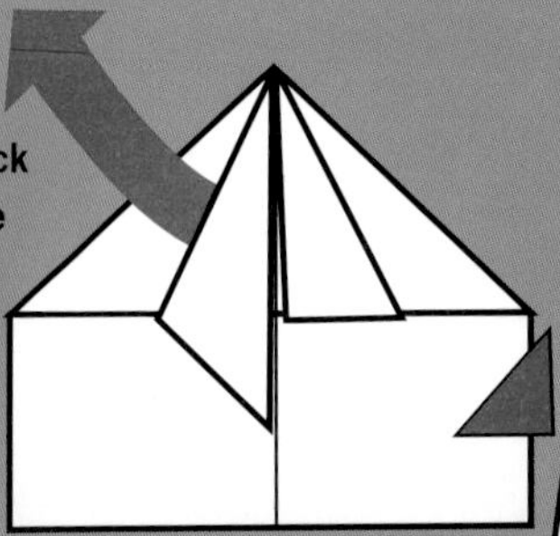

11 Rearrange the paper using the creases shown. No new creases are added!

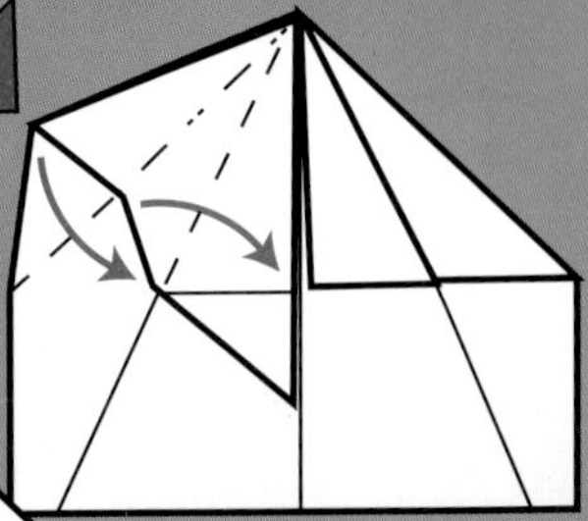

12 Fold the plane in half (this is the opposite direction to step 6), tucking the small triangle behind the flap on the other side as the paper closes. Fold slowly! This now locks the fuselage together, giving for improved flight characteristics. Refold the wings, again in the opposite direction to step 7.

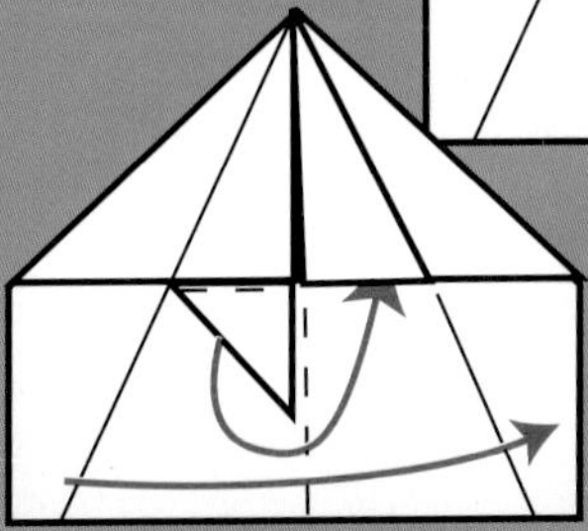

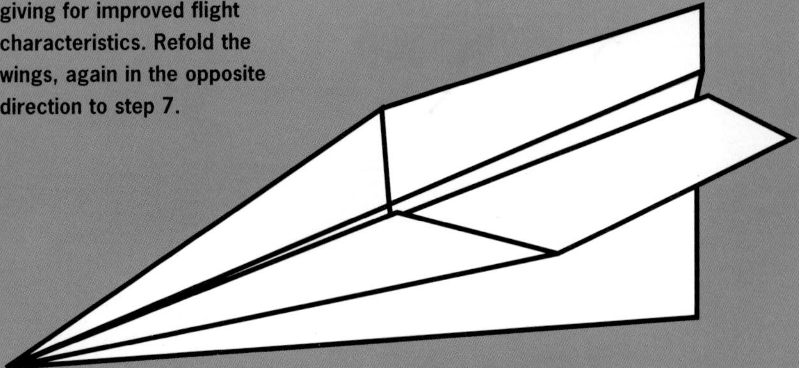

Modern Designs

Using folding techniques discovered in the last few years, these designs represent a step forward from the traditional, classic designs. Perhaps in years to come they will become classics themselves, or like the Northrop Flying Wing (pictured left) develop into something completely unexpected, like the 'Stealth bomber'.

Barnstormer

This origami design by the author starts from a square rather than a rectangle. The shape of the paper causes different design problems (such as the paper becoming too thick), which can lead to unusual and exciting solutions! The variation at the end will produce 'eyes' if you start with paper that has a different colour on each side. This is one of the designs for which there is a template supplied.

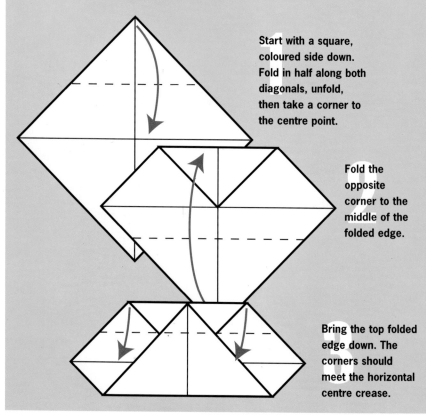

1 Start with a square, coloured side down. Fold in half along both diagonals, unfold, then take a corner to the centre point.

2 Fold the opposite corner to the middle of the folded edge.

3 Bring the top folded edge down. The corners should meet the horizontal centre crease.

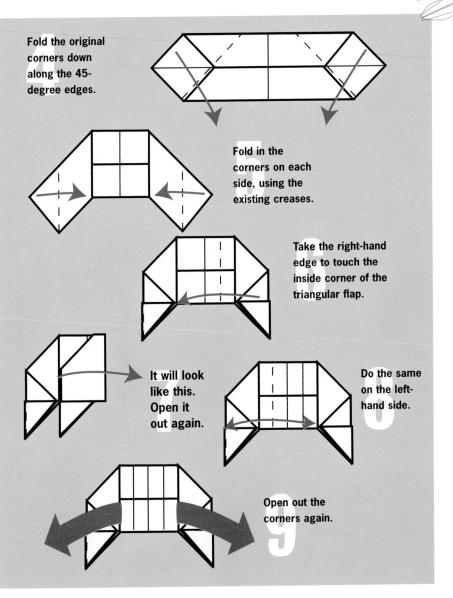

4 Fold the original corners down along the 45-degree edges.

5 Fold in the corners on each side, using the existing creases.

6 Take the right-hand edge to touch the inside corner of the triangular flap.

7 It will look like this. Open it out again.

8 Do the same on the left-hand side.

9 Open out the corners again.

39

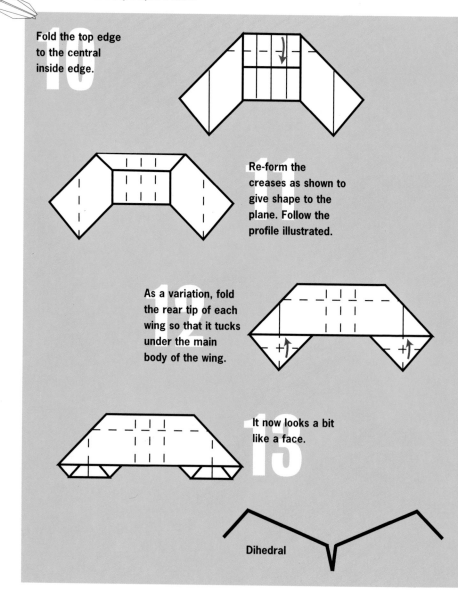

10 Fold the top edge to the central inside edge.

11 Re-form the creases as shown to give shape to the plane. Follow the profile illustrated.

12 As a variation, fold the rear tip of each wing so that it tucks under the main body of the wing.

13 It now looks a bit like a face.

Dihedral

TIPS

Try various angles of launch from straight forwards to straight up.

Try launching faster or slower. Fast launches will produce more aerobatics.

Try folding the plane from very light sheets of paper.

Triplane

This plane takes its name, not from the number of wings but from the equilateral triangle that forms basic crease pattern. Creating a 60-degree crease is quite easy, but you need to be accurate when you line up the paper in step 3. This is one of the designs for which there is a template supplied.

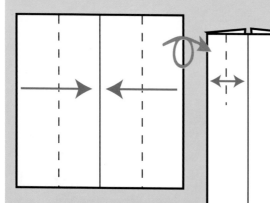

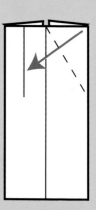

1 Start with a square, creased in half from side to side. Fold the sides to the centre and turn the paper over.

2 Fold the edge to the centre, creasing only a small section. This provides a location point for the next step.

3 Starting the crease at the middle of the top edge, fold the corner across so that it meets the crease you made in step 2. Check the next diagram to see what you are aiming at.

42

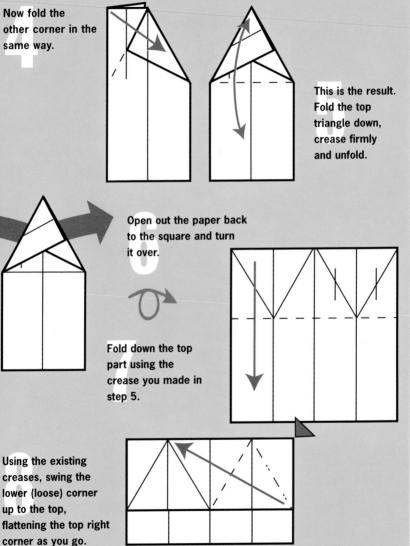

4 Now fold the other corner in the same way.

5 This is the result. Fold the top triangle down, crease firmly and unfold.

6 Open out the paper back to the square and turn it over.

7 Fold down the top part using the crease you made in step 5.

8 Using the existing creases, swing the lower (loose) corner up to the top, flattening the top right corner as you go.

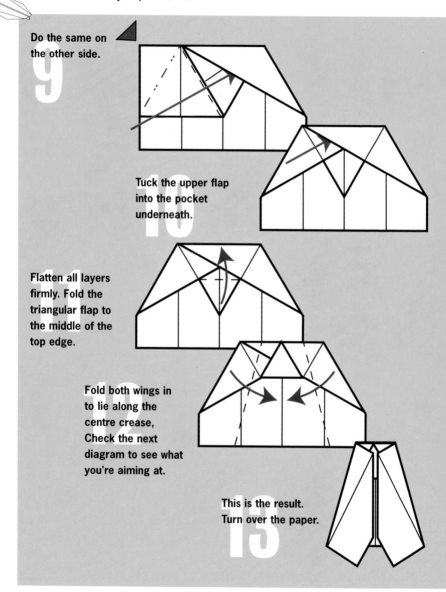

9 Do the same on the other side.

10 Tuck the upper flap into the pocket underneath.

11 Flatten all layers firmly. Fold the triangular flap to the middle of the top edge.

12 Fold both wings in to lie along the centre crease, Check the next diagram to see what you're aiming at.

13 This is the result. Turn over the paper.

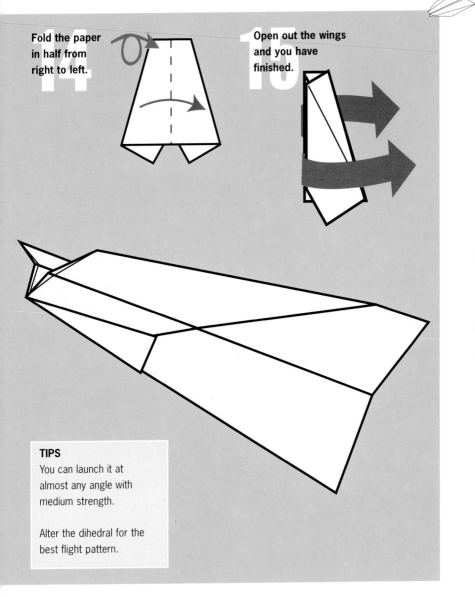

14 Fold the paper in half from right to left.

15 Open out the wings and you have finished.

TIPS

You can launch it at almost any angle with medium strength.

Alter the dihedral for the best flight pattern.

Norton Flyer

This design, named after the area in which I live, is best at slow, long-distance glides. You need to fold all creases as accurately as possible, making sure the paper is in the right place before you flatten the crease. This is one of the designs for which there is a template supplied.

Start with a sheet of A4, creased in half lengthways. Pinch the halfway point of this crease to find the centre of the rectangle. This pinch-mark helps locate nearly all the creases. Fold a corner to the centre point (marked with a dot).

Repeat with the other corner.

Fold the two main outside corners to the same point.

Fold the 'nose' corner to the same point. Try to be accurate!

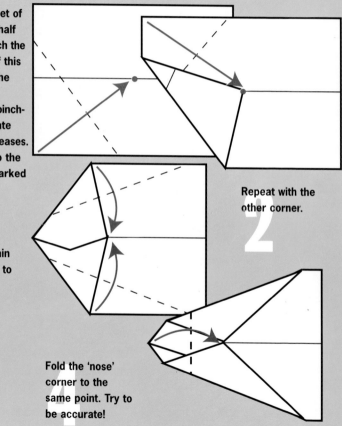

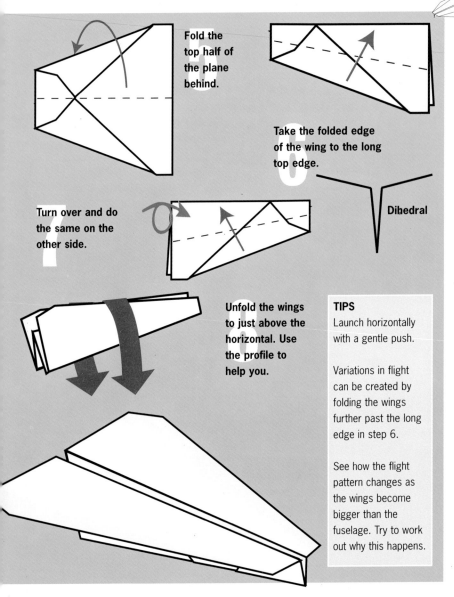

Fold the top half of the plane behind.

Take the folded edge of the wing to the long top edge.

Dihedral

Turn over and do the same on the other side.

Unfold the wings to just above the horizontal. Use the profile to help you.

TIPS
Launch horizontally with a gentle push.

Variations in flight can be created by folding the wings further past the long edge in step 6.

See how the flight pattern changes as the wings become bigger than the fuselage. Try to work out why this happens.

47

Renishaw

The large wing area compared to the fuselage, makes this a very stable, slow glider. Designed in a small village in Britain, the opening folds are similar to those in the Triplane (page 42) and also use 60-degree geometry. This is one of the designs for which there is a template supplied.

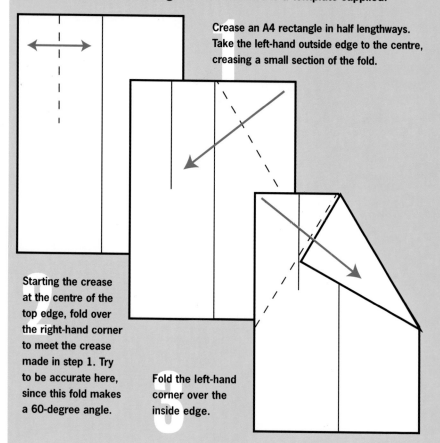

Crease an A4 rectangle in half lengthways. Take the left-hand outside edge to the centre, creasing a small section of the fold.

Starting the crease at the centre of the top edge, fold over the right-hand corner to meet the crease made in step 1. Try to be accurate here, since this fold makes a 60-degree angle.

Fold the left-hand corner over the inside edge.

48

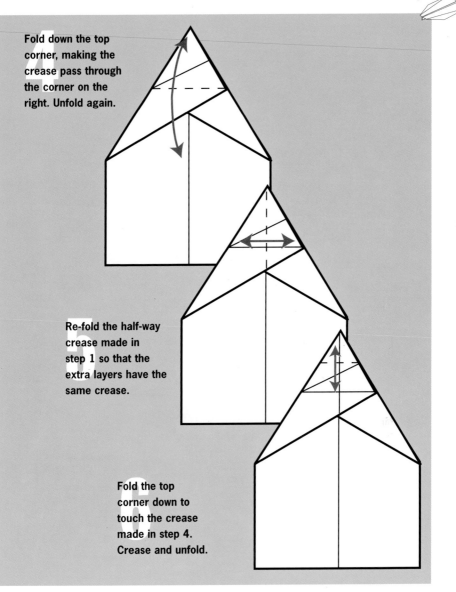

4 Fold down the top corner, making the crease pass through the corner on the right. Unfold again.

5 Re-fold the half-way crease made in step 1 so that the extra layers have the same crease.

6 Fold the top corner down to touch the crease made in step 4. Crease and unfold.

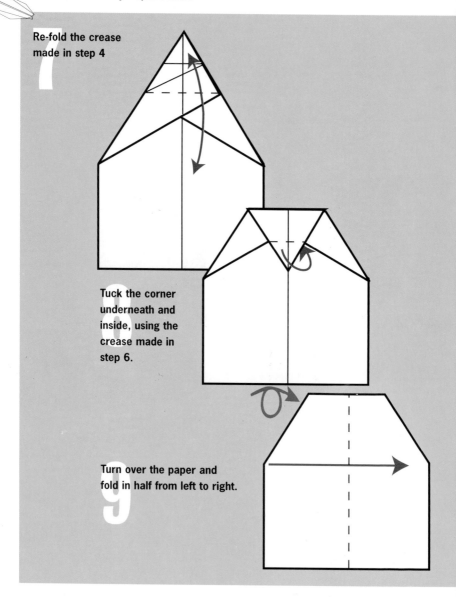

7 Re-fold the crease made in step 4

8 Tuck the corner underneath and inside, using the crease made in step 6.

9 Turn over the paper and fold in half from left to right.

Make a crease that starts at the lower right-hand corner and meets the upper right-hand corner. Try to be exact here! Repeat on the side underneath.

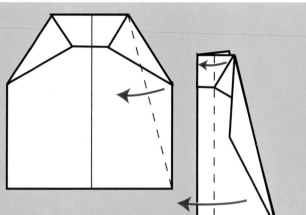

TIPS

Launch the plane straight forwards with a gentle push.

Alter the dihedral for the best flight pattern.

Dihedral

Fold both wings downwards so that the two corners at the top of the plane meet each other. Open the wings to slightly above the horizontal for the finished plane. The outer tips of the wings bend down slightly.

51

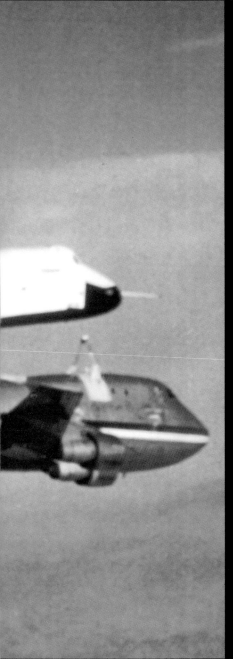

Space Age Designs

There are many ways in which a sheet of paper can be made to fly. Here are some examples that spin, twist and generally point the way forward for paper flight. Why not use your imagination and adapt some of the designs presented here?

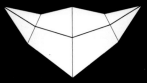

Seed Floater

The clean lines of this design were inspired by the seeds of a South American plant, which can float over 2km (1.2 miles) from the parent tree. It will need careful adjusting, but will glide beautifully when balanced. This is one of the designs for which there is a template supplied.

1 Start with a square, creased in half along both diagonals. Fold an upper edge to the horizontal centre, crease and unfold.

2 Repeat on the other side.

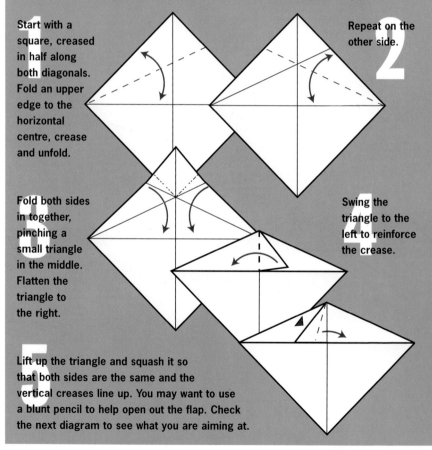

3 Fold both sides in together, pinching a small triangle in the middle. Flatten the triangle to the right.

4 Swing the triangle to the left to reinforce the crease.

5 Lift up the triangle and squash it so that both sides are the same and the vertical creases line up. You may want to use a blunt pencil to help open out the flap. Check the next diagram to see what you are aiming at.

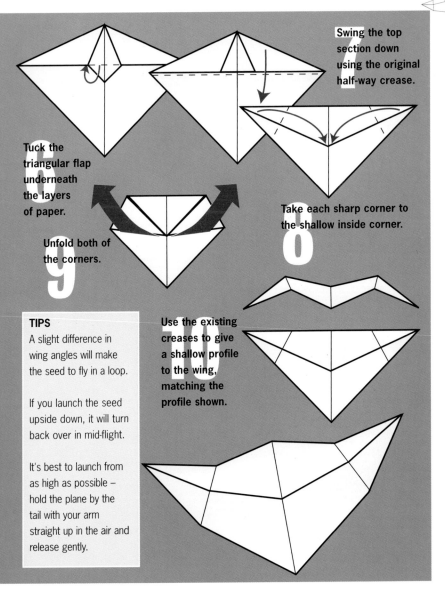

Swing the top section down using the original half-way crease.

7

Tuck the triangular flap underneath the layers of paper.

6

Take each sharp corner to the shallow inside corner.

8

Unfold both of the corners.

9

TIPS

A slight difference in wing angles will make the seed to fly in a loop.

If you launch the seed upside down, it will turn back over in mid-flight.

It's best to launch from as high as possible – hold the plane by the tail with your arm straight up in the air and release gently.

Use the existing creases to give a shallow profile to the wing, matching the profile shown.

10

Space Fighter

This may be the shape of things to come if we ever colonize space. The change of angle in the wings gives the design stability when flying in our atmosphere – wings are not needed in space!

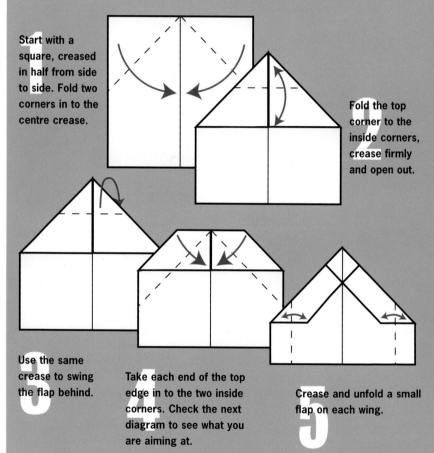

Start with a square, creased in half from side to side. Fold two corners in to the centre crease.

Fold the top corner to the inside corners, crease firmly and open out.

Use the same crease to swing the flap behind.

Take each end of the top edge in to the two inside corners. Check the next diagram to see what you are aiming at.

Crease and unfold a small flap on each wing.

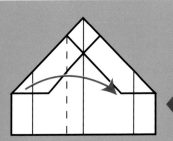

6 To form the main wing, fold so that the outside corner lies on an inside corner.

7 It should look like this. Unfold and repeat on the other wing.

8 Turn over the paper and fold the small square at the top in half downwards.

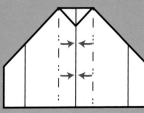

9 Using the creases you have already made, form the fuselage and adjust the wings to match the profile shown.

TIPS

Launch the plane at any speed or angle.

Adjusting the wing-tips lets you perform aerobatics and loops.

For a slow, stable glide, gently bend the rear of the wing-tips up a little.

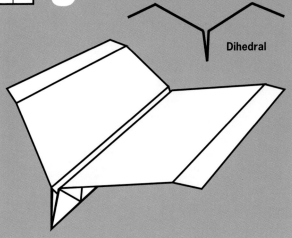

Dihedral

Roller Blade

As well as designs like the Whizzer that spin round,
there are planes that twist by pitching around in a rolling motion.
Made from bright paper, this can be really eye-catching.

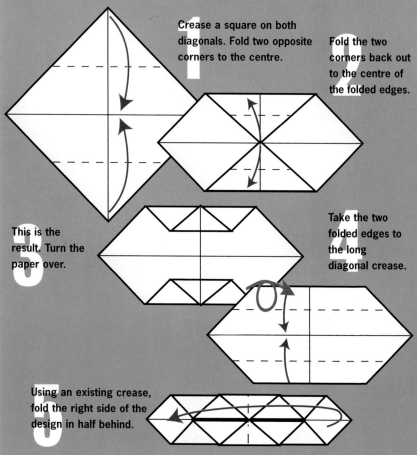

1 Crease a square on both diagonals. Fold two opposite corners to the centre.

2 Fold the two corners back out to the centre of the folded edges.

3 This is the result. Turn the paper over.

4 Take the two folded edges to the long diagonal crease.

5 Using an existing crease, fold the right side of the design in half behind.

58

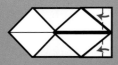

TIPS

You launch holding near the centre with a slight downwards flick of the wrist. This starts the rolling movement and as it falls the pressure of the air perpetuates the action. Larger paper will give a slower speed of roll.

The higher you launch it from, the longer the time aloft will be, but be very careful when launching it from heights.

If you make the Roller Blade from a plain sheet of paper you can draw open eyes on one side and closed eyes on the other. As it falls and spins, you have the illusion of winking! Can you think of other tricks?

6 Fold over a small flap so that the right-hand corners touch the inside corners of the small triangles.

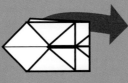

7 It should look like this. Release the flap of paper you folded behind in step 5.

8 Lift the small flap upwards at right angles to the main piece of paper.

Whizzer

This traditional design isn't really a plane, but it lets you turn yourself into one! Although the folding sequence is really simple, there is a 'knack' to making it work. Don't give up too easily; once you start flying around the room, you'll want to show off your skills to your friends.

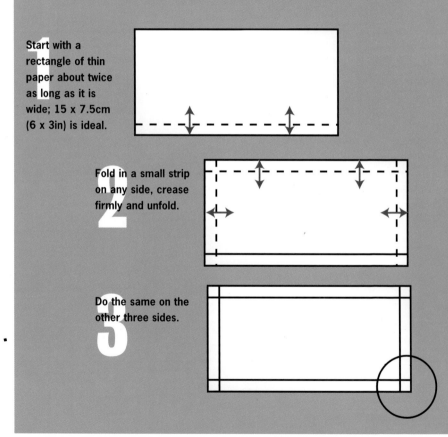

1 Start with a rectangle of thin paper about twice as long as it is wide; 15 x 7.5cm (6 x 3in) is ideal.

2 Fold in a small strip on any side, crease firmly and unfold.

3 Do the same on the other three sides.

4 Add a small crease to each corner, by pinching the paper together.

5 This is the result.

Start to walk forwards in a straight line and as the paper starts to turn, move the front finger out of the way. As long as you move at a reasonable speed, the Whizzer will stay on your finger, spinning merrily.

If you really want to make yourself dizzy, try spinning round in a circle!

See how slowly you can move without losing the spinning effect.

When you are confident, try making the Whizzer from slightly larger or smaller paper and see how it affects the flight.

Does the Whizzer always turn one way? Why do you think this happens?

Teach some friends to fold the Whizzer, then have races!

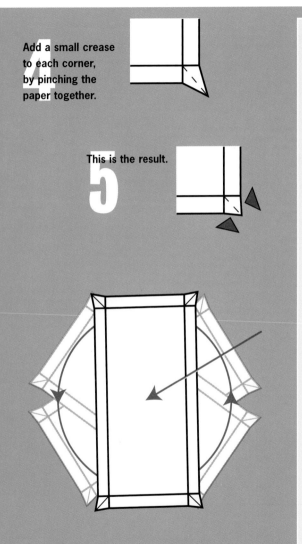

Glossary of Aviation Terms

Aileron The hinged section of a wing that controls lateral balance.

Airfoil An aircraft wing that produces more lift than resistance.

Angle of attack The angle at which an airplane's wings meet the airstream.

Asymmetrical An airplane with wings of different shapes.

Axes The planes in which an aircraft can turn, indicated by X–X, Y–Y and so forth.

Barnstormer An airplane that can perform spectacular aerobatics.

Canard An airplane with a tail on the front rather than at the rear of the fuselage.

Centre of gravity The point at which an aircraft achieves balance.

Control surfaces The parts of an aircraft that affect its flight pattern.

Dihedral The angle formed by an aircraft's wings and the horizontal.

Elevator The stabilizer on the tail plane that is used to tilt an aircraft up or down.

Flight pattern The path through the air taken by an airplane.

Fuselage The body of an aircraft.

High-lift wing A wing that creates more lift than a conventional wing.

Laminar-flow wing A wing that creates less air resistance (drag) than a conventional wing.

Lateral control The effect of making an airplane roll (turn around its long axis).

Leading edges The front edges of an aircraft's wings.

Lift The upward force that acts on the wings.

Mach number The ratio of the speed of an aircraft to the speed of sound.

Ornithopter A type of flying machine that resembles a bird.

Pitch The up or down movement of the nose of an aircraft.

Rate of roll The speed at which an aircraft can turn around its long axis.

Roll The movement caused by one wing being higher than another.

Rudder The vertical tail plane.

Stable An airplane that flies without rolling, pitching or yawing.

Stall An uncontrolled fall to the ground when the force of gravity is greater than lift.

Supersonic An aircraft that is capable of exceeding the speed of sound.

Swept-wing An aircraft's wing on which both the leading and trailing edges point backwards.

Trailing edge The rear edge of an aircraft's wing.

Unstable An aircraft whose flight pattern varies uncontrollably.

VTOL (vertical take-off and landing) An aircraft that can take off straight upwards.

Wing tip The outer end of an aircraft's wing.

Yaw The movement caused when one wing moves ahead of the other.

Index

angle of launch 17
angle of attack 13
Aristotle 8

Barnstomer 38–41
Bell X-1 10
Bernoulli's Principle 13

Cayley, Sir George 8
centre of gravity 14
Classic Dart 24–5
classic designs 23–35
Classic Glider 30–31
competitive flying 19–21

Dart, Classic 24–5
Dart, Hawk 26–9
dihedral 18

Fighter, Space 56–7
Floater, Seed 54–5
Flyer, Norton 46–7

Glider, Classic 30–31

Hawk Dart 26–9

Keel Plane 32–5

Leonardo da Vinci 8, 9
Lilienthal, Otto 9

Montgolfier, Joseph Michel
  and Jacques Etienne 9
mountain fold 16

NASA 10
Northrop, John 9–10
Norton Flyer 46–7

origami paper 15
ornithopter 8

Pilcher, Percy 9
pitch 14
Plane, Keel 32–5

Renishaw 48–51
resistance 12–13
roll 14
Roller Blade 58–9

Seed Floater 54–5
space travel 10, 11
Space Fighter 56–7
speed of launch 17

Triplane 42–5

valley fold 16
vertical take-off and
  landing (VTOL) 10

weight 18
Whizzer 60–61
Wright, Orville and Wilbur
  9, 10

yaw 14
Yeager, Charles 10

Acknowledgements

I'd like to express my thanks to various members of the British Origami Society for advice and encouragement over the years, including Lord Brill, Edwin Corrie, Mark Kennedy, David Mitchell, Paul Jackson, Wayne Brown, Paulo Mulatinho and many others. I would also like to thank Ken Blackburn for making his vast knowledge of flight available to me; my wife for being patient when I spend far too much time on my computer; my children for keeping me humble and tired; and Penny Groom for introducing me to my publishers!

The author

Nick Robinson is a former professional origami teacher. He has visited schools, libraries, youth clubs, hospitals and many other venues, teaching origami and paper artwork. He has worked with people of all ages and physical abilities, included those with both aural and visual disabilities. His favourite origami designers include David Brill, Kunihiko Kasahara and Philip Shen.

Nick has appeared on television, radio and has written other books on the subject. His original creations have been published in 13 countries around the world. He has contributed articles and designs for the British Origami Society (BOS) magazine and has served on its council for over ten years. He prepares the worldwide web pages for the BOS and takes a keen interest in computers and the Internet. As a former professional musician, he still performs live, playing solo improvised ambient guitar.

British Origami Society

For membership details of the society, please write to;

Penny Groom
2a The Chestnuts
Countesthorpe
Leicester LE18 3TL